# ENTREPRENEUR HACK:

*What it takes to Start Small to Reach your Big Goals*

BY

OLACHI 'LACHY' UZOMA

# Foreword

Entrepreneurship is something I hold very dear to my heart. My belief is that I was born to be an entrepreneur. My first business began at the tender age of 6, in the cold dangerous streets of Chicago with my little sister Kandice. Over the years, I've had two clothing stores, two restaurants, was a barber for 10yrs, in addition to a photographer and videographer for weddings & family reunions. For some time, I was DJ for family reunions and weddings. Let's just say, there was a diligent quest to find my life's purpose.

It wasn't until ABC introduced the TV show Shark Tank that the seed would be planted in me to write a book and that book publishing would ultimately be the thing that would change my life forever.

Back then, if I had the tools and information Olachi shares in this book, success may have come quicker for me.

She has taken the time to write and hand you the Entrepreneur Hack! This book is a cheat sheet to success. You see, it took me years to discover the wonderful insights she shares in this book. Things like being fearless, the importance of having a plan, how to speak well over myself and my business. I've learned all these things the hard way. Fortunately, she has cut to the core and presented you with a no-nonsense guide for entrepreneurs.

Thank God! Because of the author's words, you don't have to learn these things the hard way, all you have to do is read the book and apply the tools she so graciously shares with you.

Remember this, "Your Dreams Don't Care How You Feel! Be fearless, do the work and get it Done!"

Mr. Kelly Cole "The Publisher"

2X #1 Best Selling Author

www.MrKellyCole.com

# Content

**Chapter 1:** Be Fearless ............................................. 1

**Chapter 2:** Pray (A Little Goes a Long Way) ............ 6

**Chapter 3:** Plan ...................................................... 13

**Chapter 4:** Exercise Patience ............................... 20

**Chapter 5:** Seed of support .................................. 25

**Chapter 6:** Speak Well of Yourself ....................... 30

**Chapter 7:** Contentment ...................................... 35

**Chapter 8:** Prioritize.............................................. 39

**Chapter 9:** Invest ................................................. 46

**Chapter 10:** Celebrate Success............................. 50

# CHAPTER 1: BE FEARLESS

The sincere truth is that we live in a competitive world in which every second and passing minute is used to invent, create or innovate. If you desire to be that person - a doer, a creative and executor, you must be fearless.

There is absolutely no room for shyness when it comes to being your own boss. The word 'BOSS' implies taking charge and leadership.

Imagine walking into a store where the owner is a timid, shy individual without knowledge of what he is selling or lacking the ability to instruct those working for him. That shouldn't be you, making that decision to go after your passion ought to embolden you despite any fear. Perhaps in that scenario, you would wonder why he is the owner or even take it a step further to ask, "Where is the manager?" That's how silly it is to aspire to or delve into entrepreneurship with timidity and fear ruling you.

Fear is the incubator for missed opportunities, death of dreams and wasted potential.

A conversation with many people in their 50s, 40s and even 30s will make you realize that you don't want to be that person (that age) full of regrets and missed opportunities. Many of the most promising talents have put off their dreams for fear of failure, what people would think of them, no support, disappointment by people and of taking action. Let me tell you this - park all those fears now! They are all wrong projections and lies of the mind that need to be ignored.

Remember, you don't want to be the auntie or uncle who always laments about past glory and potentials but remains irrelevant, never taking a shot to actualize your dreams. Let that be the daily reminder if that's what it takes to shake off the fears that are standing in your way to the greatness you desire to fulfill and your life's calling purpose. I believe in your case, becoming your own boss and establishing your own business or brand, will place you at the highest seat of relevance in your career rather than a manager/employer.

## The Biggest Test

When you decide to let go of fear, beware that you must replace it with faith. This has to be the biggest challenge to truly determine if you're mentally and spiritually ready for what lies ahead or if you still have unfinished 'mind work' to do within yourself. When faith fills the void of fear, it leaves no room for obscurity and propels you to commit to the leap. Try to sort out the following responsibilities; not the opposite.

Also, beware of friends, family, and associates who will consciously or innocently remind you of the last time you failed at starting or any weaknesses from the past with regard to taking that leap. It is a test. You must strive to pass. Don't fear negative reminders or quit; Faith it until you make it and overcome with positive responses. Think of their reminders as a 'So what?' challenge. The smart thing to do is not argue or feel bad, but politely divert the conversation in a more positive direction with realistic words of action that you will fulfill.

You may have been careless with managing your affairs or completely chickened out the last time you promised to... Just do it.

Now is the time to prove to yourself that you can overcome this time around. Your friends and family may pull out all the stops to prompt you to reconsider or be convinced that this endeavor is an adventure that is too big for you to embark on. It is all part of the test.

Buckle up because this is just the beginning of an insightful journey to self-discovery. As you discover your capabilities, you discover more fears and unravel your inner strength to kill those fears. Sometimes it's like a closet of insecurities that ought to be emptied out.

Make up your mind to face fear head on in order to find the faith to start.

**Quote:**

*"I have learned over the years that when one's mind is made up, this diminishes fear; knowing what must be done away with fear." - ROSA PARKS*

*I say: "Do away with fear, kill it or it'll kill your time."*

These five affirmations will build you up to be fearless:

1. I will learn to act on my goals in spite of any circumstance.

2. I am valuable. My value must be seen rather than heard.

3. My dreams will not make themselves come true. I will.

4. I choose to believe in me enough to ignore fear.

5. I am in charge, capable and fit to do everything I put my mind to; no dream is too big. I can handle it.

When you tell yourself these affirmations more often, it may seem silly to you (the speaker) but with time you will believe it. Speak against fear and give your self-esteem the boost it needs. Whether you want to admit it or not, being fearless is the strong suit of any ambitious mind, and you are just that. Walk in this consciousness that those fears are in the wrong mind. War against the thoughts that oppose your dreams starting and giving your passion a shot. Raise your head high to advance and accomplish your goal to embark on the journey of great returns in faith.

This is just the first step in the right direction.

# CHAPTER 2: PRAY (A LITTLE GOES A LONG WAY)

The year 2016 was the most restless and loneliest year for me. I had friends and appeared to be a very outgoing person, with various endeavors on my plate. So, one may ask, "How could you feel lonely when you have so many people around you & things to keep you busy?" In hindsight, overcoming that season of my life has given me the understanding that the way you begin your year steers its trajectory. Unknown to many, I began that year with a lot of uncertainty, sadness, and bitterness. Part of the reason being, I returned to the US after a five week-long visit in Nigeria to see my mom. The trip gave me a sense of emptiness and reminders of goals unaccomplished. Knowing that I'd come back student loans on minimum wage income from jobs unrelated to my field of study, made me feel sad. On my get away trip, I could finally sleep. Of course, with 16-hour shifts for two out of seven days, plus plenty of overtime adding up to an average of 65 hours per week, reality didn't afford me that luxury. The trip to Nigeria was a get-away from my ugly reality of two jobs and being on survival mode, trying to pay back student loans with a minimum wage jobs that were not in my field of study. Besides, #TeamNoSleep seemed to be a hashtag that I boldly co-signed as my claim to hustlehood. Oh, how times have changed. Also, the monetary gifts received in Naira (Nigerian currency) were a reminder that I deserve to be showered with gifts instead of working so hard to pay the bills before I could get a gift for myself. Wow! What a stark contrast. The reality hit me like a ton of bricks.

My self-esteem, my finances, and my mind were quite a wreck as it became more apparent that my vacation that was meant to refresh my body, mind & spirit had become the beginning of daily self- loathing. I was still unable to secure a job in my field of study, and just as I got a new job in social work (a bit of a consolation since it was a similar field), I lost my health care-giver job. Soon after, I landed a second job in social work (still paying minimum) wage. All of this meant back to working crazy hours, #TeamNoSleep and #BurntOut.

However, I downplayed the way I was feeling, thinking that just being a Christian would take care of things and I failed to realize that communication through prayer to God was essential.

One key lesson that I learned was that the sooner we communicate our dreams, aspirations, and goals to God, the better for us. It certainly saves you the time to worry about what could be. God is more than able. Don't overload yourself with self-criticism and regrets of what could have been and start working on what will be. Take all your children to God in prayer before you set out to make those major moves. I truly believe the biggest and the best move you can make is the act of dedicating your agenda to God. Why? Because He knows your potential and sees your future ahead of time. He is the only one who can provide you with the tools of hope for what's in store. (Jeremiah 29:11)

As you begin to do so there will be transparency, freedom in your spirit, faith and hope built up, as well as newfound reliance on God for the ability to move forward without looking back. Prayer releases the

**8**

burden of how the building process will be done and places it in God's hands like an architect and owner relationship. So, you must trust the design model.

If you are like me, your prayer is not necessarily focused on getting ideas or asking for the motivation to start, but to help you select the best ideas that work in line with God's purpose for you.

This is what I call a 'prayer for guidance in purpose' often. The entertainment of too many ideas, wondering about conflicting thoughts, and having to settle your mind in order to focus on the one that is right for you can cause confusion. From my experience dealing with this issue, at the time, I saw it as the gift of many ideas (Joseph's coat of many colors) and embraced it as a good thing. However, it becomes pure confusion when you don't narrow your focus on the main idea or passion. In order to be a master of what you are passionate about, you must discipline yourself to become great at it before venturing out to take on others. Most of the time we learn the hard way by becoming a 'jack of all trades' without any mastery of the niche we are meant to hone-in-on. That's why guidance through prayer is needed. It will help your mind to settle on the main idea, (the one that matters most) in starting your entrepreneurial journey. It will also shield you from the pitfalls and commotions of too many ideas in your mind. Thus, helping you to channel your inner focus to reflect on your choices right from the start.

You must realize that it's on you to discipline your mind and put it under submission in order to get to a greater level of focus; no one will do it for you. The use of meditation/quiet time with God and or retreats are vital in developing that discipline.

## What is a Retreat?

It's a set time to withdraw forces in a battlefield setting, mostly implemented in the army especially when outpowered or victory has been declared.

In your case, you are not outpowered. Retreating is more for mental and spiritual centering- a strategy to fuel you before the start or refuel, recuperate and reassess, when your mind is unsettled.

## Three Things to know about Retreating

- A retreat is not a vacation. However, a vacation can be fit into a retreat if you're in a different environment (being away from your daily atmosphere can change your perspective and relax your mind to pray more).

- Retreating is necessary even when others may be of a different opinion. No one knows your body like you do and sometimes your body or mind can be the best prompter for you to take a break. Others may not see it and may advise you to keep going if they feel you're strong. There is also strength in taking a break to relax and offload the stressors of goal-getting.

- You can choose what to retreat from. As much as retreating completely from your normal routine is great, not every circumstance permits or requires that. Remember that it's not just an action but a state of mind. So, you can take a break from certain habits or practices that you have lost control over in order to regain discipline. 'Social media fasts' have been common especially with the power that it has to absorb our attention and distract us from hitting our goals. I have taken a retreat from Instagram, Facebook, and Snapchat (never went back, ha-ha) ...

Whenever there are signs that you are lacking focus or have too many ideas to choose from, rather than sink into confusion, retreat into prayer.

11

If a little prayer can manifest great things that you ask for, then a retreat has the power to spark the drive you need to meet your goals in life. So never take prayer for granted as an entrepreneur.

A little prayer is a spark to set the fire of God motivation.

# Chapter 3: Plan

People always seem to want the quick and easy route but are surprised when they get it, then lose it the very same way. Is it safe to say that desiring the quick and easy route, avoiding and scaling through mandatory planning, shouldn't be the aim?

Yes. Newsflash! The road to success takes time. It requires a plan that is carefully engineered with utmost intentionality.

Planning is not only important to an entrepreneur for the journey in business/branding, but also in developing personal habits that set the tone for a life of intentionality.

Entrepreneurs must know that there are two parts to planning: the before planning stage- for those aspiring, and the after planning- applies to start up & the established business.

**THE BEFORE:**

This part is basically the legwork and background building blocks to kickstart your business. The first moves in your plan to start a business online are:

#1: Know your niche market/specific demographics to cater to. 2: Gather practical research on what it takes for you to do so.

It's important to know that 'the before' stage is a mentally intense part that needs to be written, mapped out and gradually pieced together for your continuous reference.

On 25 February 2019, I had to come to terms with closing my shop that I had been building alongside a business partner. It was part of the before /background and planning process which took a lot of time and energy, however the decision to stop the plan was needed in order to move on to a better strategy- to sell on a more established business platform with high traffic (that I didn't have at the time).

There are many trials and errors that I had to experience on the quest to become an entrepreneur. You will experience that too, if you haven't already; prepare for them. The most essential advice you can give to yourself is to go off in the field, plan, and drop the feeling of dissatisfaction that comes along with it. Secondly, jump on the next plan with the new strategy points. In other words, life is like a dream, when it stops moving then get on another one or else you will get left behind. The before is the starting point, but the most impactful is the after point.

**THE AFTER:**

The journey of entrepreneurship comes with the desire to establish yourself in the long run. So, you must know that 'the after' planning should become second nature after reaching your first major milestone or establishing your business. They are easy to use and helpful tools that you should get familiar with:

**•Calendar:**

You should have one on your phone to track deadlines, important dates, scheduled order delivery, or reception days. You must have one on any device such as your computer or tablet. You can even have one on your desk at home with the reminders.

**•Web docs:**

This has become more modern and every business is going digital and using virtual documents that can be easily backed up. A web version is simple and easy to download, keep track of, edit, share with customers/clients, and easy to access on file from any location.

**•Hardcopy planner:**

A lot of us still have the old-fashioned journal style planners where we can visualize and know schedules and other things. Walmart knows that is important to use the make-it-plain approach to note about your day-to-day goals and progress desired along the way. There's just something divine about having them in your writing to be able to reference later.

**•Chart:**

Not everyone is analytical, but having a physical chart helps to form the habits of measuring your progress and how far along you've come. If charts can be used to record your progress with timelines in order to make visual estimates or projections in a team project, then it can be used for personal projects too. They are best when drawn out for yourself/ business partners/team to see all the elements in what you are working with. Having different ones like the pie chart graph chart for specific events helps. I remember the day I planned to launch my online store for the t-shirt collection I had created. I had made sales through word of mouth and offline so I surely thought it must be easy to create an online store and move forward. Unfortunately, as the day was approaching, I was struggling to pull it off because my plans were not outlined or carefully laid out with daily sales or even a timeline to help me accomplish my goal. This is a mistake you may have experienced, so it's important to set a realistic timeline to execute those visible steps you have written out. All tasks that need to be checked off your to-do list would always be better on a phone or app to access. If you really feel like planning is your strong suit and would like to do more in a business that specializes in planning, here are a few:

Start-up company

Event planning company

Online content creator

Professional organizing,

Project management contractor

Real estate agents

Business development coach

Life coach

Brand Marketing Strategist

Community Coordinator

Virtual Assistant

Decluttering Specialists for private practice office, Consultant as a Third-party Agent

Party Planner/Promoter

Stay-at-home Mom a.k.a. Momager

You are probably surprised to see that a stay-at home mom is also an entrepreneur. That's right! Single parents included. It surely is a full-time job on its own. Hats off to you if you are a young parent, especially if you're a single parent and work full-time. Managing kids' schedules especially when they're a bit older involves a lot of planning and patience working with high dependency. Being young and still in your prime, you may want the freedom of not having to manage the schedule of a little human since you're still trying to figure yourself out. It's possible. You can certainly do it with little or no help and your determination will show in how you plan your daily routine. Planning is hectic but it's necessary. So, get ready.

For my aspiring entrepreneurs, it is essential to draft a small business plan:

There are six steps in a business plan:

1. Choose the type or sector of business that you want to focus on

2. Carve out a niche that best suits your goals and gifts as an entrepreneur

3. Seek out a mentor or go to the company that provides similar services or products

4. Choose a resume format

5. Provide a separate document with all useful resources for the business plan that will serve as a reference for later

6. Use Google as your best friend on 'how-to', but ultimately you make your business plan your own

# CHAPTER 4: EXERCISE PATIENCE

Have you ever felt like your desperation to become a success story after so many ugly situations with being broke, broken or experiencing consecutive losses, has led you to become a 'groupie?' Don't be a 'groupie'... you are worthy of substance and just like other things of substance, success doesn't come cheap. You will have long nights working on your crafts like a student pulling an all-nighter for exam day. How about the early morning to go out and execute that plan? Yep. Believe me when I tell you that these two activities will be far from comfortable; but after doing them 'one too many times', it will become your routine in your journey. You will realize that after a while, the very same sacrifices that you made will manifest the goals and business that you desire. It takes time. Be patient in order to gain what you desire. Here are some notions you must dispel for you to allow yourself to exercise patience:

1. **STOP OVERTHINKING:** As an entrepreneur, you must think but don't overthink. Overthinking the distance necessary to hit your goals will drive you crazy. You can't afford to lose your sane mind, neither can you waste mind space by drowning in brain fatigue.

2. **THERE IS NO EASY WAY:** People make entrepreneurship look easy as 'flat lays' and stock photos (even if so, there's a lot of thought, editing, arrangement and strategy that goes into it). With consistency comes added effort and for the most part, that's what poses the biggest challenge in times when it seems efforts are not yielding instant results.

3. **MONEY SOLVES ALL ISSUES:** In present times, everything has become significant, which means that a business can start with online resources for free. With free Wi-Fi at a public library you CAN START A BUSINESS... Yah, good news, right?

Nonetheless, people still use the excuse of not having money as the reason why they can't start. They think that money is the automatic solution, whereas getting the amount they desire could turn out to be a crutch. Money can be a blessing or a curse, it all depends on your mindset of its purpose and usefulness. Do you know that if care is not taken, it could quench the fire to be a goal-getter, improvise or kill the drive to carry on with your aspirations? It's like the 'lazy rich kid plague'.

4. **YOU NEED AN INVESTOR:** (Just to piggyback off the last myth.) Money is not the solution for all, and investors are not necessary. Understanding that it's important most times, not to rally for investors but focus on investing in yourself as a brand first with free resources. It's the first step to developing yourself for the business. Self-development is the single most essential tool for investing in the brand. So, go ahead, take a course (or YouTube equivalent), do your research, associate or network with creatives now to build up your 'bank' of knowledge because you are the biggest investor you need. If anyone will take a chance on investing in your business, they will need some assurance that

they can bank on your readiness, capability and accountability, which will all start with what you have invested in yourself.

5. **DELAYS AND SETBACKS:** I know an entrepreneur who has made sacrifices, not because his success is already evident but rather his discipline. Sticking to what you believe in can be a delayed process, it is not a setback. Here's why: Let's use Steve Jobs, for instance, the founder of Apple Inc. who went from founder to fired then 'jobless' for several years; what an irony. Many success stories were characterized by failures, periods of drought and delays that were out of the control of the main prospect. Not all cases, but a great number of them are, so be encouraged.

On the journey to becoming an entrepreneur - a successful one at that - you must get acquitted with the waiting and trials of delay that come for several reasons. This surely will build up the virtue of patience that applies to all aspects of life. There's a popular phrase used by drill sergeants in the Army - "Embrace the Suck"- it's a simple catchphrase that I've chosen to interpret as:

- Endure till your reward comes

- Learn to tolerate the pain that comes from pursuing purpose

- Endearing times can also be enjoyed

- Tough times can yield enjoyable rewards

- A patient spirit can turn trials into a grateful fit

# CHAPTER 5: SEED OF SUPPORT

What makes you stand out as a true, loyal friend is your willingness to support the goodwill ambitions, ventures and visions of your friends and/ or family. It's also a trait that you should use to rate your affiliations with people. Knowing who to add to your circle of influence and who will remain on the bench is vital. If you can't make this distinction, you may end up with a crowd of associates that lack loyalty. This is a scary situation to be in. The multitude can never make up for the quality of a few trustees.

If that 'so-called' friend of yours doesn't motivate you to live your best life, dream big, live out your calling or at least push you towards it, then he or she is not "a trustee." A trustee friend is not only loyal but accountable. A trustee friend is worth every ounce of your support because he or she will go to great lengths to reciprocate your support for them by supporting your own vision.

It's crucial to know that people can speak on what they will do for you- "I'll take a bullet for you"- but still do the most disloyal things to you at the slightest test of friendship. Here is the microblog post from my Instagram, published in October 2018, "Support your friend, listen to their ideas, go to their event, share their posts. Celebrate their victories and remember failures. A little support can go a very long way in someone's life."

And if I may add, if you can, make a world of a difference for a fellow goal-getter starting out and battling with the temptation to give up by providing a simple act of encouragement to boost morale.

That same post was captioned below, Support systems are built out of love, selflessness and community...often times we ride or die and spend money to go watch our favorite sports team or a music concert that costs $200, but we can't commit to spending a fraction of it on a local business owned by a friend who has a startup or even would repost the event just to support. The reason why I am committed to supporting the small business, especially locally owned, is because they don't get enough of it.

## Perspective over Popularity

I reached out to one of my favorite Instagram pages, an award-winning wedding cinematographer, after seeing a short clip of film.

It was a strong and compelling piece that inspired me. I suppose to the common eyes on Instagram, it wasn't the typical material-like comic skits with profanity, which gets more attention. Our conversation lasted for about 20 minutes and we both agreed on the need to change that very morning, by taking a step to be the change. Also extending support as part of the movement to encourage other creatives that may not be popular but possess good quality content that sometimes goes unnoticed. We also could agree that helping those within our reach is more rewarding than celebrities outside our reach.

*"Celebrating others is a seed of encouragement that is greater than any money you can give a friend."*

Celebrate, celebrate, celebrate. Celebrate what you desire in ALL its forms. What a good heart space to start the week.

Celebrate the friend with the big promotion.

Celebrate the bestie moving into her dream home.

Celebrate the friend falling in love.

And the one making amazing changes to her health.

And the one who's energy is as bright as the sun because she's working for it.

And the one who makes time for creativity.

And the one who makes time to clean.

And the one seeing new heights of her company.

Celebrate the woman on the Internet with the unstoppable voice.

Celebrate the celeb with wildly successful art.

Celebrate the politician who's trying. Really trying.

Against all else.

Celebrate the mothers, mothering.

If you want it, and they have it, you've got to find the delight not the denouncing.

*The kind that goes, "God, I don't get what people like about that." Or, "They only made it there because of x/y/z."*

*Or, "That won't last." Or, "That's not how I'd do it." If you want something in your life, you've got to celebrate everywhere you see it. Because it's coming for you. It's a practice of gratitude. It's collective abundance. It's yours...."*

@maxiemccoy

# Chapter 6: Speak Well of Yourself

Have you ever felt like you were a positive speaker and the kind of person with uplifting words for a weary soul, but then as soon as you experience a season of challenges, your speech changes? Just as thoughts of negativity and self-doubt settle, what you say about the present may not have any visible impact on your immediate outcome, but it can almost certainly haunt your future. This was the case when I wrote a short post to encourage anyone that may have been going through a hard time. To my surprise, a high school friend of mine sent a direct message to me, expressing how much that post meant to her. Following that was another person who called to air out sincere feelings about relationship issues and the constant struggle to stay positive through that experience. So here I was again encouraging her not to give up, be strong, and only make positive confessions irrespective of the reality. However, after that call, I had a mini meltdown in which I felt alone and began to entertain negative thoughts. That was totally opposite to the advice that I gave out on social media. Does that make me a hypocrite? Not at all, sometimes we have to say (in this case, write) what we hope for and instead of contaminating others with the poison of our current situation, resort to uplifting them with the hope of a better situation.

In 2017, when I had just made the move to a new city, I kept applying for jobs and finally landed a job on the spot with a law firm. It felt like everything was finally falling into place as I had envisioned but it was only short-lived. Here I was again, back on the job market without a job in a new city that was supposed to create better opportunities than I had experienced previously.

After what seemed to be misfortunes, I began to look down on myself and think that maybe I wasn't enough, and then this kind of negative thinking slowly leaked into the words I'd catch myself saying. This scenario is right around every corner and can be the case more often than not in situations of difficulty, hardship, misfortunes and failed attempts at pursuing your dreams. You must not only look at yourself in the mirror and say words aloud words and make positive confessions before the day starts; but also say words out loud to counter your feelings. Affirm yourself EVERYDAY, EVERY STEP OF THE WAY AND EVERYTIME another person tries to ignite or trigger self-hate.

**SAY THIS WITH ME:**

*"I am brilliant, I am outstanding, I am a success story, I am an over achiever, I can do all things because God who created me says I CAN, my life  may not be where I want it now, but I'm better than yesterday, I'm a healer of my own wounds, I choose to love me, I am worthy of love, my mistakes will create a miracle, my mess-ups are a part of my success story, great minds were once uncovered like me, so I'm a great mind reaching my discovery. I am making MAJOR MOVES; I am a leader and visionary..."*

Write these out, say them in your car on the way to work, in your garage/dream incubator/business storehouse), after your first sale online or even when getting out of bed seems so hard. Why must you do this constantly? Just as your nutrition reflects on your body, skin and other elements of you, so do your words reflect your mindset and vice versa. So be careful with your words. Do not to say the things that can poison your mind, alter your path and stunt your growth as an entrepreneur. Be brave enough to speak life into a gloomy situation of failure.

I truly believe we are a product of how we affirm ourselves through the power of our words. Just look at me; I began thinking and saying that I'd become an author at age 9/10. What started as a liking for storytelling has turned into a love for writing and much more. It truly takes confidence to speak in faith beyond what is the current reality; however, when you master this, more confidence builds, you become more hopeful for a greater outcome. Over time you will attract people who speak the same language of optimism and create a circle of great influence.

Too often we remain stuck in the budding stages of a solo career aka entrepreneur starter because of negative speech. Oftentimes focusing more on the success unreached and forgetting how far along we have come on the journey. Speaking well of yourself will elevate your confidence first, then your status as a beginner because people who encounter you will believe your words and treat you accordingly. Your words are one of quickest ways to make an impression and state your purpose in any interaction with others. They will know that you are not a regular degular person.

# CHAPTER 7: CONTENTMENT

Heading home from my seasonal job as a bridal consultant, I began to reflect on how I had gotten to that point. I was working a retail job that only payed ten dollars an hour and worked a total of 12-25 hours a week, with bills stacking high and I had unpaid student loans. That night as I drove, my thoughts wondered so far away as I looked at my fuel gauge indicating empty and the engine & oil check lights were on as well. The car gradually slowed down till the car behind me honked so loudly and woke me out of the blank stare of worry. Then he sped up to meet me at the same stop light where my car came to a halt. As I flagged other drivers down for help, all I could think of was who I could possible call that wouldn't make me feel like a bother. In that same moment the thoughts of how discontent I was with my life began to weigh heavily on my mind, and the cold breeze of spring that blew across my face as I stood by the sidewalk of a major road. Then suddenly to my surprise, the same man who was honking at me out of annoyance from the slow and inattentive driving showed up. He and his girlfriend parked in a business center parking lot just to help me push my car out of the road. He said, "Hey, you seemed like you could use some help." As I replied with relief in the tone of my voice, "I definitely need help." My sarcasm was restrained from reminding him that I noticed his earlier impatience. They loaned me a phone to call for help and the first name that popped in my head was Mr. Onu. The couple was kind enough to wait with me for an hour before help arrived. I noticed that they had a car full of personal belongings with pillows on the headrest and blankets in the passenger seat. During the time I was with the 'good Samaritans', he began to share a story of how he had a job working for a construction company until immigration services started investigating the company to fish out illegal workers. Although, he had been with the company for many years and had his documents to work, the company was dissolved because most of the workers didn't have their papers. This left him without a job. That began his struggle with depression and alcoholism. He then joyfully said, "I'm so proud of myself that I'm out of rehab and six months sober." On the other hand, the lady who had a said, "I'm lucky to have him sober (she laughed). Even though we're homeless, at least we have each other." This particularly struck me as a lesson, that although I had come up on hard times -in debt, working minimum wage and a car with issues; this couple had it much worse than I did. If a person living out of his vehicle could find a way to be grateful and kind, then I could use that as an opportunity to be grateful.

Often, we are not content, especially with the dream or vision of how we want our life to be at certain benchmark age. It's okay to want more for yourself and push yourself to meet life's personal goals but never forget what you have in front of you, which is life and some change. There is a difference between persistence and being hard on yourself. You must find balance in your persistence, in order to avoid going overboard. As an entrepreneur, you are goal-getter and often times will find yourself in a phase where you have to regulate the 'over-achievers' syndrome. The pressure we put on ourselves to reach our goals at all cost, within an unreasonable stipulation of time/deadline is what I've tagged as the 'over-achievers' syndrome or too-hard-on-thyself.

Take a second to smell the roses. After every run is a stretch to relax the muscles. So, if you're constantly checking and balancing your progress with realistic expectations and considering circumstances and change of plans, you will find yourself becoming content. I will never advise anyone to be satisfied with a mediocre life and especially not an entrepreneurial mind and goal-getter with big dreams like you. So, find balance within your drive for success. Those big dreams of yours will never allow you to leave any stone of opportunity unturned. I'm almost certain that you will not rest until you see every vision and plan come to flourish. However, that is no guarantee that times of complacency will not try to creep in. So, it's safe to say that contentment is the balance between the two extreme levels in your journey as an entrepreneur. It will reflect your gratitude for goals accomplished and those yet in the future. It will be the reminder to stay sane.

# CHAPTER 8: PRIORITIZE

Hello fellow entrepreneurs, you cannot possibly do all things that you want without proper prioritization in place. First things first, get your priorities in check. There are two parts. One, Knowledge of what is most important. Two, planning to create the lifestyle you desire and future you love. Prioritizing is applicable to all aspects of your Life- personally, professionally and publicly. Additionally, planning items in order to suit your lifestyle and future. Also, it affects aspects of your life. 1. Personal 2. Professional 3. Public life.

### • Knowing what's important:

Assuming you have things planned and have already lined them up in a journal with the aim of checking them off as accomplishments as you go... Before you continue, ask yourself this question, "What's the #1 goal right now?" This is just the start of greatness and knowledge is key. So, this question will help you sort out your short-term goals as you go down the list from 1-5 in order of what is most urgent. Then the next will be to outline the long-term goals in no particular order, preferably within a 5-10-year marginal timeframe.

When you write them out it makes it easier to refer to and remind yourself to stay on course. As time goes on, challenges will come but knowing what's important will help you to fight off sidetracking agents.

Placing them in order to suit your lifestyle and future. In this sub-section, it requires you to split them up:

### A) Personal goals

These are goals pertain to what shapes your personality and makes you an individual. For instance, my personal goals in high school involved learning how to save, being an outstanding student and learning to be confident to interact with people in social settings. Ha-ha, ohhh the basics of teenagers. Then in college it changed to balancing work with school to pay bills, student leadership involvement, community service both on and off campus.

## B)  Professional goals

These goals are the umbrella for career aspirations and keep you constantly reminded of where you are headed as a professional, climbing the corporate ladder or saying cut that crap to start your own business. If you think that making A's in all business courses in school determines that you will be successful in starting your own business, you are mistaken. Most times your learning experience is in that 9-5, handling and managing another person's business. Most times it's when you are being treated like crap and your talent is either underpaid or overlooked, that the spark to ditch the 9-5 job to venture into what you're truly passionate about, is ignited. That experience always serves as a reminder when you decide to 'GO FOR IT' and along the line want to quit.

That's the reason we should always write down that day for later reference (it comes in handy).

Many of us who are entrepreneurs have had that mindset or always aspired to become one, even as kids. We did not know that was a professional life goal.

I remember as early as eight years old when I would spend hours jotting my feelings down and although it was all over the place, something in me knew that was my passion - WRITING!

Although it got me in trouble many times when others would find my stories or raw thoughts, I continued because it was my confidence as an introverted and shy kid.

As time progressed, I wrote more. It was this passion that eventually scored me an internal document at the court where I worked as a research/evaluation intern for my last year in college.

It all began with scribbled thoughts and here I am writing my first book almost two decades later.

Useful tip: Your professional goal to be a CEO/founder or public figure will require the beginning experience of being an intern or entry level at 'a job' so be patient with the process to get to the top you desire. Set your sights farther but respect the process by making it a major priority to do whatever it takes to climb up. Write down your goal to become that CEO or person of significance, knowing that your biggest priorities are not just floating in your head but have a sitting place in your planner, diary or device for continuous reference.

Your public life is the part of your life that you choose to expose to the world. It has a lot to do with shaping and projecting your image as a person of significance and/ or brand. In setting goals for how you desire to be projected, it may be of concern to you that they are realistic and not a clone of how someone else (not even your mentor) views you. Your small business will become big someday so take into consideration that what you stand for or support while it's at the small stage could be challenged when it becomes a giant company. Your public image will be affected adversely if you don't set it up for the future.

For instance, motivational speakers, authors, or most public figure (brand bio) labels on social media don't make you a role model. However, it's expected that when you have a platform with a wide reach, there is a moral obligation to do well and stay away from scandals. Many business owners, public figures, and the alike have been blackballed because of distasteful actions that tainted their public image. It's certainly a killer of destiny and purpose.

## Summary

So, while the first part of prioritizing focuses on urgency and time capsulation of life goals, the second part is a more specific and sectional listing that focuses on the three different aspects of your life.

## Why is this important to do?

Order! Without organizing your priorities, there would be chaos. How you organize them is vital to the journey to accomplishing them. You understand it better as you go through and follow the steps. There's a special sense of care and attention to details attached to those who prioritize or organize their responsibilities early on in life. This is because doing so is really time-consuming. Keep in mind that it's already a great challenge as you try to juggle all the things you have to do daily.

So, you can imagine how much dedication and discipline is factored into prioritization for those who are in college, raising a family or may be a single parent. One thing is for sure, you cannot afford to make excuses or quit on your goal of building your brand/ business. Remember the source of your goals- your mind and determine in that same mind to prioritize your way through the process.

**Quote:**

The most important nugget to take away is that "*EVERY IDEA IS NOT YOUR PRIORITY, BUT WHAT YOU PRIORITIZE SHOWS YOUR DESIRE TO EXECUTE.*"

# CHAPTER 9: INVEST

On the 18th of February, I met a guy who sang along to a Christian song that I was singing to, so I asked, "You are a Christian right?" His response, "yes, a broken Christian" …. which prompted me to ask what he meant by that, which made him share with me how he had 24 arrests, three DWIs and two fatal accidents that sent him to the trauma unit of the ER and several rehab centers. His first prison sentence was a few days after his 18th birthday. In my mind, I was so shocked at his life experiences at the age of 22, I shared some words of encouragement that were relevant to his struggles, but beyond that was how we could both agree on the fact that his wrong choices resulted in years that could very well be deemed 'wasted years.' The opposite of 'wasted years' or opportunities are invested ones. The greatest investment that a person can ever make is in themselves and their future. For you to fully be able to do so, you must fearlessly and wholeheartedly choose yourself every day in the scheme of priorities in life. Choose to put your passion and dreams first no matter the cost that comes with it because no one can do it for you like you would for yourself. They are probably busy doing that for themselves.

I once had a discussion with a mentor about investments and tough choices in business. During the discussion I asked this question, "How can you put yourself first as part of investing in yourself without coming off as a selfish person? "The response I got was very simple and straight to the point, however based on personal experience, I have been able to detail it into tools that are helpful such as:

1. Find your mile base on your passion and focus on building up your knowledge bank with that in mind. You can find online courses that provide you with basic intermediate information that you can start off with to develop your skills in that area. If you want to become a freelance photographer, you can find out about different equipment needed to start, techniques to use,

thereby training yourself with the assistance of tutorials and other free materials that are accessible on the net. This can help you determine the specific kind of photography you enjoy and put your skills to practice and grow.

2. Realize you are a better resource to others when you have the means from within. If you don't have what others are looking for or need, then what good are you to them? Those around you would have to realize that the things you do to invest in yourself are meant to be a threat or disadvantage to them but rather your way of empowering yourself to empower, inspire, influence and to be a resource to them. Only those who do not have your best interest at heart will see your self- development as selfish. Don't stress it. Do you.

3. The sooner you build for yourself, the closer/further along you get to future success. The worth of a man is truly embedded in the actions he takes to attain a fulfilled life, living out his dreams/aspirations and impacting others. The journey can consist of failures, years of drought, lack of recognition, major losses and even attempts to give up. All of which takes a lot of energy, so it's important to preserve that

energy for the journey and focus on building your strengths to fight the urge to quit and avoiding associations with self-centered people who may leach from your energy and not consider your needs on the journey to entrepreneurial success.

If there is one thing you are should take away from this chapter, it is that your success in life as an entrepreneur is directly linked to how much you invest in yourself. It is part of strong foundation essentials that good quality cement bricks or blocks are used to start the process of building a ground home. In the same way, a strong foundation is essential for a successful life as an entrepreneur. It is the good old-fashioned way of taking that time to do all the things that add up to build, shape, increase your knowledge, establish your confidence and develop you in your given mile of business. There's no fast track or crash course. You have the key to build you up and time and experience will tell. You can truly become the expert you dreamed of with the wealth of what you have invested in yourself.

# CHAPTER 10: CELEBRATE SUCCESS

In 2015, I had just graduated with my bachelor's from the University of Arizona. That year marked my 6th year living in Arizona, and far away from my mother. So as expected, it was the biggest accomplishment since leaving home. The celebration was a decent get-together with about 50 attendees ranging from student leadership to affiliates within the local community. In the months leading up to my graduation, I remember being asked by a family friend what my plans for graduation were and how I was going to celebrate it. He asked, "Anything special like a trip or party?" The response in my head was, "Why should I celebrate, when I'm broke and wasn't able to secure a job at my court internship?" However, I resorted to give him a simple answer of "We will see how it goes"! Truly in my mind I was just glad to be hitting a milestone of finally graduating. For God's sake I made it. The point that I missed is that it's not just enough to be grateful to finish or check that off the list, but also not to forget the journey.

A celebration or a hurrah comes from a place of reflecting on the hard work that it took to make it to the finish line. Celebrations are both statements; they leave a moment in time and give others the opportunity to rejoice with you. Such a big milestone, whether I knew it or not, deserves to be applauded regardless of the GPA, merits, awards, or job security.

I was so focused on overachieving that I didn't realize how much I deserved to be celebrated. There's a popular saying that "If no one celebrates you, you should celebrate yourself." It's a very deliberate move, and with the right intentions, will not make you appear to be a show-off. Dare to be deliberate but put those intentions in check! In today's society, where comparisons are easily made, the wrong intentions can push anyone to celebrate falsehood or be motivated just to prove a point. These are attributes of a show-off. Don't be that kind of person. You would lose appreciation for your uniqueness, the essence of celebrating you.

Also, remember that your celebrations along the way show appreciation for your support system as well. This shows that it's not just about you but those who have helped you on along the way; it says a lot about your personality- a bold person who knows who they are, no matter what others may think. You're in a competition with only your old self. Start with the small successes, you don't need 100K followers on Instagram or one million views on YouTube to consider your efforts celebration worthy. You may be a beginner, but you won't remain that way forever. Just know that the energy you invoke with your gratitude for now, will attract greater progression for what you will become.

Sometimes people look at you like 'what the heck is she celebrating for?' or 'didn't you just celebrate that already?' or maybe think you're just a show-off. Will you leave it up to people to dictate what you celebrate, or will you do it anyway because you know your value? It's up to you to decide.

Here's five reasons that ought to convince you:

1.  It shows your gratitude to those who support you. You may not think so, but people are

watching more than they are buying. It's important that they see how grateful you are for their patronage or support because they're not just buying what you are selling.

2. You are as courageous as a go-getter. You've experienced self-doubt and had a very large share of fears, now you found the courage to venture out of fear into faith. A person like you is doing what many couldn't do.

3. It starts with you. Tell me, how do you expect others to celebrate you if you don't realize your goodness to celebrate yourself? Have you ever heard where it said that if you don't love yourself, how do you expect somebody else to love you or what you do? Go Getter Behavior 101: love what you do. Celebration reflects self and the seed that keeps going to your efforts towards your accomplishments. When you are a bully doing this, you'd be surprised how the song will catch on. The community around you looking up to you could do it first. If you are an entrepreneur, you may be the only one in your community who is black so celebrating your diversity makes you stand out.

4. Celebrate the little and greater it will come. Your humble beginnings would be a reminder of how far you've come, when you hit your success markers and continue to expand. Don't despise those little milestones because they are valuable. The late nights, early mornings, last-minute emergencies and overstretched budget that come in the initial stages of building the foundation deserve an applause. The strength to persevere through the times that nobody witnesses will be showcased for the world to see.

5. Keep it moving. People are watching you develop. They see you grow little by little and although they may not be sure if you will stand the test of time, that's not for you to worry about. Don't beat yourself up on how few supporters there are or feel like you're tired of proving a point. Celebrate now because sometimes all you need for you isn't to focus on others, but rather yourself. You can give yourself a little pat on the back, but don't get too comfortable. Keep it moving.

I overheard a conversation of two parents comparing the achievements of their children. Quite frankly, it's a norm in Nigerian society to do that. If you find yourself in a position of doing things that do not fit your purpose for the benefit of earning your parent's celebration, then maybe you need to reassess the reason why you aim for what you do. You may find yourself alone. Celebrate you, celebrate your dream in spite of who is or isn't in support. Celebrate yourself despite the boxes you are yet to tick off on the list of expectations anyone may have. Celebrate your dream as you fulfil it bit by bit because YOU ARE JUST ALL THAT!!!

Best Wishes to you Goal-getters, now go out there and create your own SUCCESS STORY.

www.ingramcontent.com/pod-product-compliance
Lightning Source LLC
Chambersburg PA
CBHW021509210526
45463CB00002B/963